WINTER FERRY

POEMS

❖

ELIZABETH ELLIOTT

Elizabeth Elliott

WINTER PRESS
TAVERNIER, FL 33070

www.eelliottpoetry.com

First Edition, July 4, 2008
© Elizabeth Elliott, 2008.

This book is printed on acid-free paper.

Library of Congress Cataloging-in-Publication Data

Elizabeth Elliott, 1932-
    Winter Ferry: poems/Elizabeth Elliott. – 1st ed. p. cm.
    ISBN 978-1-60585-277-5 (alk. paper)
    I. Title.

Cover painting by Evelina Kats

This book was set in Adobe Caslon. Book, cover and CD cover design by Kat Moran, Windfall Designs, Stuart, Florida

Website designed by Faith Englund, Stuart, Florida and Diane Zeigler, Montpelier, Vermont

Audio CD mastered by Greg Steele, Derek Studios, Dalton, Massachusetts

Published in the United States of America by
    Winter Press
    Tavernier, Florida 33070

In memory of

Donald Oakes

*who asked the right question
at the right time*

❖

WINTER FERRY

❖

O N E

Winter Ferry

He had been one of the old men who worked on the docks,
had a hundred stories to tell, and did,
he talked to us now amid the dry shafts of flying ice,
amid the way to go forward,
with only the compass keeping steady.
He said, "What came over didn't necessarily come back."
Nor was it all one with him.

He sometimes told of being home,
of the Scotsman she had married
when it was too late and the accident too near,
not that they were any Tristan and Isolde,
they were both older than berries left on the trees for birds,
and she was not, as they say, "she of the white hands,"
but the color of royal.

He said, "They called her Aubergine,
she came from across another channel, not ours;
she was delicately spaced in vowel and flesh.
Already survivors of at least one blast of month-long sleet,
she cleaved to him as though forever had been found,
though he loved to tease and say he was the first
to see and love, the first to know 'always'."

But here again we saw land
and knew he'd warned us truly,
that what had crossed
would not, necessarily, cross back.
Too late now. For them. The usual disrepair
of some past glory

1

brought them down together,
not just to the quiet street they knew and where they were known,
but fallen to the Dragon Pen of cliff,
to gravel the rivenning sea had not yet hobbed away.
"Their bones are still down there," he said.

"Bright talent that other one as well. But Mestre fingers
pinched upon the atlas of an expanding world
and he sold himself,
got run in for a line of cocaine snort
when he'd been poised to try for more."
He said, "Boys who saw that mountaintop cave in,
turned to trees no bigger than a poplar limb."

Gravel on a hook of land,
deserted even then of boats, a boy gone bad.
"Like a bright talent that land once was."
And he swung the wheel hard left
to bring us back to center as the ball in a tornado
strikes past the target. "Our children froze in unearned fame,
a slingshot tabloids made to bring the giants down."

Again we sighted land, and until the clouds skewed in again
to knead us in a death-soft vise, saw land again,
then land still further on, beyond any mile,
and we knew we had no destination.

"Oh yes," he said, "once we all had faces that were real,
but they have blurred to the discard of histories."
And what had crossed
would necessarily not return.
The night kept coming on,
no eye could melt the layers of that rich ice,
ears drummed to accessories of black wind.

"But then there were the pears," he said,
"the pears and the blue, sea-washed glass. Shall you hear this too?"
His voice was light, "That fall day three of us went down the grade,
heading for the level tracks beside the river,
we nearly passed the field, a very small bit of turf it was,
just big enough for six trees,
six pear trees and every one had just then dropped its fruit."

A prolonged weeping came scudding off the bow and when it slowed
the old man was still in remembering, "The grass was yellow with ripe fruit,
unbruised, clean from rain, not yet pocked by hornets or the southbound birds.
There was enough for a month of juice and skin,
and how we pressed it to our lips. I loved that smell, not like any other,
pear, ripe for the mouth and thirsty tongue.
What I wouldn't give to taste it now."

Too crazed a howl streaked from the frost-filled ghosts,
winds baying like trapped or abandoned beasts
wrapped in grief that could neither save themselves
or tip us over into hell. We lost the inside of our own minds.

When the winds had cast themselves another way,
he was still in his inward pause, "So generous the way things used to come."
He spoke as though we did not know this also.
His story now was of an island beach gone ankle-deep in sea-washed glass,
" — though blue, sea-washed glass by then was rare,
plenty of brown glass, yes, and clear glass, and plastic of every sort.
But no longer the blue, not until that morning.

"The dead girl had been compared to the blue. After the service
we looked for a quiet walk and climbed down a nettled bank,
expecting to find a beach of Maine's own gray stone,
but found ourselves wading in blue, sea-washed glass."

He paused, conjuring, and the boat ran steady in the waves.
"It lay deep and peaceful as far as our eyes could find a beach,
it covered every rock, and was only a deeper blue where it found the tide."

"We had fields of harvest then," he said, "and our daily crossings
were only for supplies. Everything seemed normal,
as if no other way existed. Nothing seemed miraculous."
He pulled the wheel toward the center and gently repeated to himself,
"It was all miraculous."
Later he spoke once more, "We weren't required to do it all at once,
just one serious gesture. We were too spoiled."

Jericho Bay

In the long and lovely lay-awake of summer,
when the distance of the sea is laid to rest,
when miles are a handful of stars away,
 and the far bird's cry leaves an echo in the stillness of the west,

when the vast divided elements of heaven,
have come malingering in the dark,
then the drifting ghost of a sail slips by,
and a haunting song cuts short in the pillows of the ark.

Now the hills beside the shore come down,
to lean into the ripeness of the ready sea,
to teach the endless liquid caverns
with the granite root of cone, dark husk, and tree.

In all such lovely moan and silence,
a universe with time itself denied,
where breath whose breathing joy is sealed,
brings stars conjoined upon the catholic tide.

Thus in our days' down-drifting toward death,
forget for now the pain of what comes after,
let green love throw its sudden bush of sparks,
let night catch forth its kindle time of laughter.

Questions From Migration

If a bird, flying with a lesser moon,
sees clouding in the sky ahead,
great majesties in peaks of dread,
gobbling her sky of promised stars,
assembling their fountains for a storm:
spin-drift, rain-wrack, wind-tear and rift, the bars
that will hobble her flight-path, this sky-night's gift —

and if this is not one bird but thousands,
have they rehearsed how to let storm rage safely below?
What are the by-pass strategies carried in genes?
Wing higher than this moment's thirty-thousand feet?
Dive and bear the brunt too close to waves and killing sleet?
Violently swerve east? Or west? Be over India by dawn?
When Morocco is the place to which their genes are drawn?

Or do they switch from their familiar system
into one so deep at their birds' safe core
that only danger stabs it to the fore?
The earth's magnetic core. Core too profound
to notice any storm's most violent brew.
Is this where birds will turn? What birds will do?
And we. Where turn? What do?

Creating The Beach On Which We'll Lie

Queen Helmet is a find,
as is the Lightning Whelk,
but mostly, sharp eyes pick out at best
the Long-Spined Star,
or, as we lean to reach,
the Common Fig, Shark's Eye or Crown Cone.

We tramp along, our sandaled feet
creating sand from Bleeding Tooth,
Flamingo Tongue, Baby's Ear or Common Dove.
Even the Atlantic's Sundial is ground to make a path.

Must the Stiff Pen,
in undimmed lacquer of silvering blue and pink,
let drop from off its nib
its every drop of life?
So that it too,
may become our beach?

Fief By Fief

Head kerchiefed in snow or neuro-surgery,
fur neckline scooped by glacial slide,
earth suffers silently the perjury,
    turns not to those
    in whom she can't confide.

Wind-whales in fields of wheat,
don't know when wheat goes mainly into beef,
but across the ice fields, sheet by sheet,
    the Arctics liquefy,
    fief by fief.

Knee-deep in trees great mountains wade,
their roots as secret as a city thief,
a mountain cuts its teeth on every glade,
    the Arctics liquefy
    fief by fief.

Peril

Call down the stairs and hear a voice reply,
"Know all is well
despite the thrashing at the gates."

Despite the thrashing at the gates,
the stricken cries,
call down the stairs and hear a voice reply,

"Know all is well,
no harm will touch the ones I love,
for none be well till all is won."

Call down the stairs and hear a voice reply,
but was it his?
Or some imposter breaking through the locks?

I hear the ringing of alarm,
some scoundrel in the garden groans,
call down the stairs and hear no voice reply.

Call down the stairs and whispers of the dead
draw close and pale lips smile,
"Know all is as it is; know all is well."

Hear the thrashing at the gates,
know all is lost, a quelling of all light.
The strongest are the soonest dead.

continued

Despite the voice that comforts with replies,
all now hear the thrashing at the gates,
know mothers in the garden with their milk,

are dying of their purple wounds.
I would descend. I would escape.
The dying stab the living to the heart.

The strongest are the soonest dead.
But stomached with intent
I will descend, be buckled into flight,

refute the voice that comforts with replies.
The garden will become the grave,
and every past endeavor mocked.

Shouts of triumph mingling bloods,
"Know I am here amid the thrashing at the gates,
You think you are immune. All do."

Let no one call downstairs, get no reply,
no garden is a grave and none be well till all is won.

Time That Was Given Us

When the time that was given us is gone,
and the wild shaking of the wind is here,
why do you rear up, look back?

Why see again the fields,
their stubble ploughed for upland rain,
why see the thistle and the grapes that climb unchecked?

Why see the road
that carves ravines, descends, arrives,
and forks and forks again,

until the tiny capsule that you made
is all that's left of any light? What drives you back
into this story, unlearn its proof, the very one you wrote?

When it is all too late
and darkness takes the wind, too late
to rearrange, reverse, repeat, deny,

does the solitary,
dimming mind demand
to understand the truth? And why?

T W O

One Particular Morning

I have not the wit, my imagination is far too dull,
to imagine anything, anywhere, at any time,
to be as pure, as peaceful,
as stepping into the salad garden at dawn.

The leaning towers of lettuce gone to seed,
the mesclun thinned by appetite,
isolated beds of mint with soft, furred eyes,
and paths measured carefully in feet
of three or six or nine;
the morning air is sweet with dew
as last evening, drowsy was with wine.

This world around,
fragrant with the sound of birds,
is all I need to imagine Heaven,
though I will never find the words.

Being

In
dark
shells
bestir
seed
of

us.
Then
behold
terror
runs
in

us,
away
beyond
flesh's
fear
of

se
par
a ti
on.

In
loss
entire
appear
self
of

an
Adam
before
fabled
Eden
in

us
bore
dreams.

Become
unto
us.

Black Cat

In dirty tall spaces, in the sturdy privacy
                                   between
a black cat,   lofts,
oiled
by the sun,
deigns

motionless to wait; the frail tame light
                                   adheres,
then courts   retreats,
again;
rich
murmuring

in fur; it eventually drops and fails; no flirt,
                                 this is
sleek cat,   no game;
no slave;
when cat's
garbs,

her daubs of gold, fall dim, the nib of her
                                 black
moves;   tail
a bawd
would blush.
No blame.

Unknown Of Birds

for the sculpture of Joe Wheaton

We stand among an unspeaking flight,
these wings about to extend, but how?

In a language of words?
In the notes of repeating song

in the air on which they float and bend?

*

We stand among all possible birds,
who may choose to relax into dance

but are poised for the blink of a bend
and a flex of relief from posing in trance,

wing-measured on notes to ascend.

*

We stand among the unknown of bird,
whose thought is of thought

as it swings to our gaze,
unknown treasure of unchartered range

unless measure by measure, word by word.

Round As A Chorizo

Round as a chorizo,
Sweet as a shrimp,
Tossed with grits,
I made a nice child.

Long as a shopping list,
Fiery as pimento in the eye,
Generous as jacaranda in full bloom,
I made a crazy girl.

Inconsistent as the wind,
Consistent as a ripening fig,
Useful as a pair of shoes,
I am a woman.

Notes From The Seventh Decade

Here's a riddle on the nature
       of being blind:
the more I see the less I see.
       It comes about like this:

I'm old. I know a lot. I see.
       I paid my dues.
But what I can't see
       is this that's part of me:

I can't see the coarse white hair
       growing just below my chin.

          *   *   *

I can feel this hair, this misplaced
       bristle from a hogback brush.
I feel but cannot see. They can.
       All those young. They see that sticking point.

Now who is blind? I'm wiser than they.
       I'm their leader in a sense.
They know they need to see
       what I can see.

Yet they can see what I can't, this palpitating
       insult to my otherwise perfection of a face.

          *   *   *

I realize I'm the only one with thoughts like these
        about the perfection of my face, I mean.
Forgive me. I'm just so used to it.
        I've held its hand through many trials.

I stood by it when we were down and out,
        when it was sick. I can't see why
it won't be with me to the grave. This daily care
        for something other than myself has taught me love.

Love always finds the beloved to be beautiful,
        an imperfection merely proof of being made by hand.

                    *   *   *

I know there are lovelier faces.
        But if we had to spend the day apart,
me on business, say, — and if in the afternoon
        I happened to get in a subway car,

and see my face already standing there,
        her back toward me,
hanging on a strap and squinting at the ads
        for birth control (a father with six little boys

laughing around his feet and he's saying,
        "Their mother says they're too much for her"

                    *   *   *

"what about me!" I see this ad and fume.
        No wonder children grow up in a rage,
"Don't those people know that we are
        the born light of the whole world,

"the glory of its bounce and beam,
         the haystack of its rise and fall,
the tender stems that buck the stream and carry
         the eggs on to the next village?

Have they forgotten that? Yet they complain.
         Those peoples. Always thinkin' me me me!")

*   *   *

Anyway — if I saw her, my face, standing there,
         reading this wicked ad,
swaying in the roar and buck
         and stopping at Canal,

and she was tired, say, and started gazing down,
         and say I noticed, near her, the youngest
and most loveliest of face, the freshest
         skin a puppy ever licked,

the bluest eyes the stars fell in,
         the straightest nose, the curviest lips,

*   *   *

and hair to make an ordinary 99 cent comb
         tremble so with pride
it would snap in two from plastic rapture,
         — if I saw her next to her,

well, it's easy to see how I'd feel.
         It's only my own dear face,
come upon, like that, unexpectedly, only it
         would make my heart rise up like bread

and yearn to see that she be well
        and safe forever. That younger face?

        *   *   *

Youth has no chance against age,
        not when love's involved;
youth seems kind of silly, hopeful,
        one wishes it well and admires.

Perfection then, this face, with of course
        the one exception, the one
coarse bristle I can feel. Perhaps I could ask
        my daughter to pluck it out.

But no. The whole chin is soft with hair.
        A meadow to remind me of some few years ago.

        *   *   *

I remember the way I used to feel
        sitting in a field,
waiting for him, feeling the soft grass
        like this — along my cheek and calf.

Now that I think of it, there were those
        who thought I was kind of silly,
hopeful. I know they wished me well.
        It would be nice to say hello someday.

I wouldn't ask my daughter anyway.
        She's getting blind like me.

At The Clark*

a query of artists

You painted a girl arranging her hair,
luncheon by the sea, the cliffs,
children, and unloading autumn's wood.

You had time for everything and the will to argue style,
to insist to serious and to laughing friends
what certain vision best conveyed new form.

You argued for impression, the changing light,
for vivid colors or new pastels, for palette knife or brush.
You painted whatever you saw nearby: a blonde bather,

a bird held by a girl dressed in Algerian costume,
the bay of Naples, ships dashing, crowds at peace,
Vesuvius puffing. You painted from the Pont Neuf,

from the cathedral-close in Rouen;
rocking in a fishing boat near Nice;
you painted a spring you'd seen before.

Men sat for historic family portraits,
women held letters from their men,
letters disgorging a hot and less historic side.

This woman was so impatient for his words,
her cape, edged in fur, is half flung across her chair,
her right glove is tossed aside, the left still on.

*The Clark Art Institute, Williamstown, Massachusetts

But the anticipated letter has been thrown on the floor;
a peasant smirks behind her chair, concealed
among flowers painted on the room's required screen.

You saw this as your brush stroked the velvet of her dress.
Was there a story here of you, of her, so eager in her gloves?
Always your unfettered mind found time.

Beauty was not a function of selling, a function of power,
it was just beauty; it was a permanence you assumed.
Your world was still the world your mothers knew.

At the time, of course, you were the new.
Your work displaced the declarative landscape,
the definite kings in definite ermine robes.

War as a pastime was over. War as a means was over.
Napoleons posing in uniforms were over.
Death comes along, of course, but power is bridled.

No wonder crowds move slowly in these rooms.
They recognize your work as if you'd painted "home".
They whisper, point and nod their heads.

Sadness and regret are in their eyes, they turn away.
They hardly move. This is no entertainment,
no clever cover-up to put an unfamiliar pain to sleep.

They vaguely realize that all they need
is for Sargent's "Woman With Furs" to be safe.
She may or may not hear judgments against furs. It doesn't matter.

She can change her coat if she wants.
She can move south if she likes.
She doesn't need to walk through snow,

the woods dim beyond the field,
the sky nearly empty of its winter light.
She can do what she chooses to do.

All we need is that she be free and safe, her lips closed,
her eyes dark with concentration on her world.
We used to look for "home" in our antique past,

in the Virgin and Child in a landscape,
the Master of the Legend of Saint Lucy,
the Cross, the Stoning, the Lamentation.

We used to take heart from the Musical Angels
playing away for the mother and child. The human family.
Its stories. Two thousand years ago. And still the same.

But the antique world urged us to accept one corner,
one corner of a field so wide with flowers and with grain
no single corner could ever have contained the Only Truth.

The scent of holiness continues to surprise and to elude.
We find it in ourselves and we find it among your images:
the snow, the farmhouse and the garden, the swift ice to the eager skates,

the portly couple crossing the boulevard,
the riders, the wrestlers, the dancer stooping to tie her shoe,
a child in reverie beneath her mother's comb.

A black magpie is perched on the open gate.
The woman, concentrating, is still crossing the field.
The "world as home." Is safety then, the only text required?

The Sitter Confirms His Portrait

You can hear it breathe.
    Yeah.
Unh-huh. Unh-huh. And it sort of shakes.
    Yeah.
It sounds so happy.
    Yeah.
And yet the two parts never touch.
    I know.
It works so hard and sits so still.
    Yeah.
It doesn't complain or need to know.
    Yeah.
And yet it can't even stand.
    I know.
There is nothing to stand on.
    I know.
It's been nailed up.
    Yeah.

He Who Walked The Edge
for Hart Crane

How can they not think of him who walked the edge
and fell, flagging the churning sand,
aware of silence as his ship drove on?

How can they not see him changed, transformed
into every shell that washes to the beach unmarred?
How may their hearts contain composure

when Gulf's every drop knows his erosion, his erasure
from the dry world; dry hearts, their fickle-sprinted minds
gape and soften with a son they can control,

but turn from him they can't,
turn from pain and opportunity
letting their only star slip into starlight,

beyond their stern, their deadly hold.

I Am The Green Tree

I am the green juice and vine outside the window of a crypt,
I am the wind that lifts the curtains and the covers and the clothes
and shows forth the clear glass and its views, the treasure in the closed chest,
the naked man beneath his beautiful masks and his suitable linens.

I am the earth on which a foot may rest its full weight,
I am the earth in which fingers and calm hands may toil,
I am the water to bear the ship and be cleaved by it,
I am the water that will change and have its own will.

I am the water
and in the evening you can divest yourself of masks and linen,
slip over the edge and dive deep into the unknown darkness,
roll and squander yourself in delight, be washed and refreshed.

I am the salmon that rides in from the sea,
swimming against your current to spawn near your source,
for you will hear poetry, see beauty and have ambition,
embrace with joy the pain of truth and cast your own shadow.

Unloose the cord that binds the furled landscape of your soul;
you will map it for purpose and for treasure,
nail its colors to a crossbar and see it flag down the day,
you will chart your maps beyond the harbors that you know.

I am not safety, I am fire and grief and sunlight on the decks of a long voyage;
my stillness is the stillness at the center of movement,

my peace is the peace of water pouring from a large jug.
You are my royal younger brother whom I have known before.

You are my elder brother who can take my hand
because he knows where it is.
You are half the fruit on one tree, half the nails in one bed,
half its lumber, its carved embellishments, its pillows and covers.

You are half its singing and creaking as of ships at sea, half of its dark tumble
and dominion over continents that have not seen it where it stands
near the last throne, where it stands in the green meadow
under the green tree, of which you are half its fruit.

THREE

Buttons

Certain words,
like buttons on a dress,

       maintained their normal role while you were here,
       though I confess that one was there unseen,
       hidden in a fold upon my breast,

       but when you turned they each came loose,
       and all, in stress, came crowding to my mouth,
       incapacitating throat and tongue;

       it was less their need of new employment,
       than their total lack of preparation,
       their training having been for separation;

       so now, in need, they did not know the rules,
       of being first or last, and especially did they lack
       the flow of being grouped along a space;

       all this rose and caused my suffocation,
       the weight of chill upon my body' skin,
       for suddenly I knew that some fine garment,

thin and bright,
was falling falteringly to the floor.

Long Live The Dog!

No! Do not say because their love
        did not outlive the bare March
        when it was mooning full,
that it now be called another name than love!

As soon say the dog groans,
        rolls over against the peeling wall,
        then struggles up and rolls again,
but is not, despite groans and long hairs, a dog.

Whoever said that June would follow March
        knew bodies take claim
        if throat lets the full stop outlast
the qualm that growls it back.

No mere lust but grave glove,
        flung down and denied until flared,
        and every finger flames root
at heart's choke to show visions both burn to die.

Twilight and evening star,
        the coil and red last clutch of suns
        spent hard to gorged land — till June
quickens both to a sated peace. The dog lives.

Love: Subject & Object

Scholar I'll be
of kissing
in the hollow of your neck.

Fledgling I was
puzzling in
the cover of your hands.

Bird I'll be
nesting in
crannies of your loins.

Kitten I was
sipping on
the sweetness of your skin.

Tiger I am
for gorging on
fathoms of your lips and eyes.

Professor I am
recently committed to
the study of what's wise.

Plus:
variations of how love lies.

Robbing The Rose

Plunder me as the bee plunders now this rose,
      hear the sizzle in its joy, huge work,

see where its body turns and turns,
      guzzling the pollen to its every part,

      robbing the rose
of that which it must lose. So rob me

      of that which I most wish to lose,
and in the losing gain what I most choose.

Rings The Mermaids Wear

What we lose by day we take back by night, and more,
for tidal contradictions of two differing minds
subside when rocked by heat the body lends
to thwarts, stems, and sterns where we are moored.

The bowline holds though words that friends admire
come cold with piety to offend,
and the subtle instinct to be open or confined
refuses to distinguish truth from rings the mermaids wear.

This dailiness of breach and joint,
the salty lather that peels the paint,
persists with both abandon and constraint
until each of us, accusing, makes fast his point.

Is this some sudden shear that cannot shake our core
as long as everything we lose by day returns by night and more?

Problem Of An Answered Prayer

Preserve me from all intense desire,
from the turmoil sometimes named as "love,"
preserve me from the loss I too much fear.

Preserve me from all those ecstasies
that catch me up and fling me high;
protect me from my near and dear.

Preserve me from the soaring joy I seek,
experience of boundaries at last dissolved,
preserve me from resumption of an appetite made clear.

And once this prayer is granted?

This sticky peace, this summertime contentment,
this lugubrious hum of flies and ripening plums,
this pitiless heaven of a shelter

is but a grave, a state of anesthesia,
a retreat into a milky womb,
a toothless swamp of health and sex.

Shed me of its loving arms,
unfill my stomach of all this food, unhinge my brain
from its benign repose; forgive me peace.

Even In Such Bondage We Are Free

The force that binds the quark and anti-quark
is no stronger than the force that lifts a fork
to lips grown supple for every torque.

Down through our tunnels DNA winds
and what it creates over time we must find,
amid forces which know how contraries bind.

Take My Hands

Take my hands,
your back's been waiting for their warmth,
for the breadth of palm,
the questing thumb;
we share a pillow so take my hands in the dark.

My hands hang here,
for me,
as the tree
from which the fruit is gone.

The vacuum took more strength
than you have had,
was the shock enough to loosen the lid?

You are the fruit of my tree,
I the fruit of yours,
the juice runs down through pits and skins.
Take my hands so nothing will fall.

Take my hands to touch the stars
and the strokes of paint on space;
the night unwillingly lets you pass,
use my hands to close the window in the hall,
please take my hands in the dark.

From The Cemetery

A comforter at my feet,
should a hoar frost fall,

a glass of water from the water table,
should a thirst appall.

But no chance of seeing you,
even if I manage to behave;

it sure would make a difference here,
for one night to share a single grave.

From Where I Sit

Some say
when you take the exit,
pay the toll,
and start on that highway north,
you'll finally see the face of God.

But from where I sit,
I'd rather wrap my familiar leg
around the legs of the one I love,
with my familiar arm on flesh
as warm as his and his as warm as mine.

I haven't felt up to God for a while,
I can wait to hear those trumpets blow;
until I get done with love right here
the only show I anticipate
is between the both of us. Keeps us out of trouble too.

The exit and the toll won't disappear,
and there's surely comfort in a traveled road,
that bumper to bumper flight to heaven;
but earthly love and earthly flesh
is all of heaven I need just now. God knows.

❖

FOUR

Plagiarize Beauty

Plagiarize beauty!
Plunder it for long sentences of hill,
its caesuras of valley filled with cloud,
for the pour of adverb as water courses into reservoirs and lies still
while secret syllables carry it underground
to the oratory of New York, to its scheming rhetorics,
the stations of the cross growing sideways into grammars we might understand.

Powder beauty in deft vellums
onto the despair that beds down on concrete,
powder it into the wine of adultery and the rich will look up and be unafraid,
menus will sparkle with words of pity and hope, daring and joy.
Pencil beauty into every atom that holds a glass of water safely in their hands.

Pull staves off the circling moon,
catch the notes as they fall, new stars singing a new firmament,
sing the song of the girl in Iraq who played in the chapters of her own trees,
learned the novels of her mother's kitchen with no glass to stun.
Oh, plagiarize beauty! Refresh the libraries of our sorry world.

Nothing Postponed

Thinking madness, thinking it separate,
believing he thought it there, apart,

he raised himself on the skis, buoyant,
and the great bridge curved over him
like a hand held loosely enough,

and he was not mad. He carried the cans
to the prison gate and was not mad, and he carried the cans
away from the prison gate and was not mad.

He carried the same cans always,
the only one on a track he knew he carried the cans
and was paid to carry. And for a clear, free time,

in the second before he became mad he knew
madness itself as present to each in equal presence.

* * *

Something always breaks in a move,

a crack in the frame
that supports the primitive, unsigned ancestor
appears after the papers are signed and the movers have left.

continued

A bent joint that appears on the stage as a curve,
causes the arm to fall softly, rippling the skin,
and the hand is positioned to reach him.

An acquiescence not seen before as ordained,
is now seen as the only natural thing,
as fame or death, love and the power of loss.

In a move, nothing postponed.

Backwards To The Start

What is this idiotic drive
to make each act
perfect as I go when all I need to do is what I need?

I don't need to clear each crust
of ice and snow.
All I need is one hole big enough to let me see. If I go on

like this I'll hook the shovel
in the new wipers.
I'll wrench them till they buckle in a rain, no use to me.

If I go on like this I'll scratch
the paint and rusts begin.
So far, the only reason I'm thinking of a new transmission

instead of a new car is because
there's no body rust yet.
Woman, get in, it's more important to see if it will start.

Once I get the motor going
the defroster will help,
the space will clear. So: will the key turn or bend?

Is the door-lock jammed with ice?
Pull off my mittens.
Dummy, you're holding the house key. You think you're perfect?

Their Vehicle

They drove it

alongside the abandoned track
until the shoulder of dried grass

became too narrow.

Then they got out
and pushed it,
one of them up front,
leaning hard against the frame.

When the shoulder
had narrowed enough
the hand on the wheel
pulled sharply over and down.

Their vehicle swerved right.

It had enough momentum
to go over the bank

still moving forward.

It was the still
moving forward
that later was said to
impress observers.

continued

Eventually
it rolled.

After it had rolled,
once, twice,

it fell,

skidded, fell, and lay against
some very young trees.

The wheels stopped their revolutions.

After a little while
they turned,
and walked back
along the shoulder

where the old grass
was now freshly broken
into long tracks.
No one was there to see

when the very young trees

gave way,
got their necks split back.

The green blood splintered, the spines snapped.

The vehicle
then rolled
the rest of the way
into the gully.

Beside Herself

She was "beside herself,"
who was beside her?
How did it happen
that she found herself
and found her self beside her,
alongside, nearby,
connected, clinging,
impossible to shake off?

When she is no longer
"beside herself,"
where, exactly, will she be?

It is too soon to close the books.

Annunciation

The body shapes itself
comfortably in and out of fashion;

if she was the only virgin you could find,
why didn't you at least knock?

Didn't you see she was reading?
Her mind elsewhere?

Or was that order from Him,
that fling out of Heaven,

that rush of your own two wings,
the only thing on your mind?

Not that you forgot the message;
but when her body drew back,

when she looks up in alarm,
might you not have said, "Fear not — "

Or was this how He learned
to do it better next time,

in the fields, under the great stars,
a baby bawling down the hill?

It was from then, interrupted at her book,
we learned to see her as alone.

To be worshipped
is not the same as being loved,

and yet how tenderly loved she is,
whether she is in, or out of fashion.

Sue, Folding Shirts

How many times have I climbed these stairs,
pregnant with clean clothes,
trusting no toy lies careless near my foot?
How many times stood sorting in this hall?

Four children all busy at the school,
with not a thought of what I do and why,
nor have I thoughts of them, of where each sits,
speaks, hides his head, or laughs in play.

> How clean the separation, yet every shirt,
> each pair of socks or pants
> brings some small wearer to my mind.

This skinny here who loves to talk, leans
restlessly on me or on my chair,
his brother commands I watch his prowess on a game,
the third just looks and smiles, goes off to draw.

The youngest is always ready for a lap,
her hands are quick to pair the socks,
quick to raise a skirt in peek-a-boo,
quick to snatch her father's shirt and run.

> Why do I see their father only in what she does?
> Not see him as for myself,
> how he would look at me, how smile, how speak?

I do not fear I love the children best.
Of course, I'm with them most!
Perhaps the separation between him and me
is incomplete because, in actuality, we're one.

Thus as I sort the socks he's by my side,
as I greet the littles coming through the door,
his love for them is mixed with mine,
as when, much later, we share Jim Lehrer and wine.

> I do not wish for wealth or fickle fame,
> it's what I have I pray remains the same:
> the voice of love in all the speaking of our names.

Long Leash For A Long Day

Whether you pause at a hydrant
designed for use in putting out fires,
or a lamp post
designed for light in the midst of dark,

or a bus stop
for use in moving, whether to where you want to go,
or away from where you've been, chosen to have been, forced to be,
and whether just this once, "please, we need you," or "I need you,"

or "I order you," or, (go back three windows, now),
forced to be because there was no other place you could be,
and so you'd been forced to stay but now you move —
At the very least you need a long leash for a long day.

* * *

Whether you pause for rich man, poor man, beggar man, thief;
(though in our culture, it's more apt to be,
doctor, lawyer, merchant, chief; soldier, sailor, or even tailor,)
count the buttons on your shirt because:

the dog who trots beside you on his leash is actually your GPS,
and if you sigh and sicken, scowl, complain,
stay or leave, demand or pray, (stay in this window, now)
he'll be the one to let you know,

how much it costs and who will pay,
but he'll never tell you outright where to find relief.
Nevertheless, don't omit to acquire
a long leash for a long day.

Listening To Bach's B Minor Mass

Tottering Angels,
>   safe behind the clouds our minds
>   are not unlocked to see,

shrink back, continually stained,
>   spattered by our puddling filth
>   which they are disempowered to prevent.

*   *   *

Once before, a high, musical,
>   brilliantly schooled and civilized people
>   added to the terrible silence.

A silence harvested from fear: a poisoned seed.
>   Angels observe the advent of something else.
>   (Have they always known or did they too, learn?)

*   *   *

A weedy harvest,
>   reaped from a departed time
>   has left us entitled and in shame,

ungathered to cry "Stop!"
>   We are separate, whether poor or rich,
>   divided, poor from rich.

*   *   *

Either way unschooled, our minds
            collapse and drown in drivel they produce,
            publicized as "growth" or "art".

My own silence whips
            in steady staves to Heaven
            and Angels are disempowered to break through.

FIVE

Three a.m.

A moon-still night,
with sense still dumb,
handle by handle Leonora treads her way down.

The odor of wild roses pours through the open doors,
the prow of lawn is lit by the scholars,
their nibs of light striking the lines.

Up, sideway and down
each glows and ebbs,
geometry of fireflies.

The fire flies indoors
with the roses.
The freight blocks.

She staggers, slides up, step after step.
Bugs chew and saw the winged house.
In her absence the moon has greened.

Fireflies through windows come and go,
the furnace bellows,
the freight goes crashing away.

Fireflies, roses, freight.
The comings and goings of sleep.

Where Is My Color?

Where is my own color?
Why was I not dipped, blessed and risen
to glow with others,
to delight the relief-seeking eye,
incised in the multiple browns of nature,
in the pigments of soil,
colors of bark,
root, brick, copper,
bronze of the great bells,
shred fire danced in the gumbo limbo?
Why am I not the pearl of the young beech?

These are the scaffolds for bloom,
for copious shade, needle and leaf,
the scaffolds for wind, rain,
for the breathing of gods.

Why was I left undone?
Unnicked in the first dye?
Parched now,
spackled in routine white?

I drink color in awe.
But I drink it from outside,
I cannot enter the mahogany tents
the chestnut and yellow tents.
I am empty of all that gift.
I thirst for the skins of earth.

Princess In Her Own Life

I go to meet my enemy
because the morning has wrapped its arms about me
and my enemy makes the morning dark.

Who is my enemy?
It is my father who comes with toil
and does not say he loves

so love has pinched itself away.

I go to meet my enemy
because in the blaze of noon the fawns have run
and my enemy obscures the running of the fawns.

Who is my enemy?
It is my mother who comes with toil
and says she loves me so many times

love is a word I cannot keep alive.

I go to meet my enemy
because the evening casts golden fingers through the grass
and my enemy blinds me, I cannot see.

Who it my enemy?
It is myself who comes with veils
of finding fault in all I see.

Bowing low, the world closes my door.

Virtual Voice

Punctual as the onset of the flu,
nevertheless, the train will not arrive.
"You have. Congratulations."

You'll need to wait.

But the train is obedient being something else.
You turn and find the station door is locked.
The gates of the galvanized fence has barbs.

It makes the local thieves recoil.
What is there to fear? The quantum breath?
A fog? Ghost-lit by a faintly-speaking voice?

Congratulations

Click for a no-fee interest on any account.
Click for no interest in any amount.
Click for taking charge of free-range change."

Is it the tape or squamish in a darkened mind?
Why do tracks head straight for the Federal Reserve?
No bends for the bends or the bender I deserve.

Conclusion:

The punctual and reluctant train was loaded up
    and switched to a town that may exist
        on a map perhaps hand-colored by a child.

    The child and you, train, town and fence,
   click open, activate a virtual night,
no matter what reassurance the screen provides,

        no one dares,

no one mentions the pearly fright
of foggy breathing
and a merely virtual light.

A Question For Darwin

When we don't adapt, we lose, that's clear.
But when a change is apt we hold it dear.

But why should we agree with "chance"?
"synchronicity" is closer to a truth.

For all of us, either word describes necessity.
But "nudge" may be truer than them both.

Reluctantly scientists now ask,
"What went on before the Big Bang?

What existed there before?" The question's vast,
required. The rest of us are practical.

Our lives make clear we must adapt or lose,
and, with a nudge, we believe in what we choose.

Put simply, when choice is apt we hold it dear,
but also: if Mystery is vast it's also near.

Arouse The Sheep

Arouse the sheep!
Wipe off your best sermons!
The planetudes of stars
graze the edges of Eden.

Arouse the sheep!
The strongholds of desire shift,
new ways need room
for new lowering of the bars.

How can we awaken to so much?
How take in the discourse,
the requirement for depth
in each and every word?

How shake the meaning of "strong"
until its jewels and its sins
pry open the mouth closed,
hard, on the spine of force?

The time for delay is over and gone,
the time for new love is now,
though we tinker on the edge of doom,
we will wake in Eden from sleep.

Villanelle For The Recurring Power Of Wind

With arms flung wide the ancient windmills stand,
    still noble and austere each vane,
    each by gentle breezes gently fanned.

But pliant minds the decades spanned,
    construed worlds deaf to a wind's refrain,
    (song sung from arms flung wide). The windmills stand.

Bypassed, but to the discerning eye as grand,
    romantic as all historied remains,
    and still by varied breezes gently fanned.

Gentle, wayward, rough or wild, unmanned
    by neither storm or sleet in park or plain,
    with arms flung wide the ancient windmills stand —

— as though some early eye in secret planned
    to instill a vision for our future gain,
    and show inspiring breezes still untiring, fan.

With classy dress new windmills dance the land,
    the harnessed winds together sing to vanes
    for whom the deathless breeze still fans.

With arms flung wide, the necessary windmills stand.

In Praise

Who would have thought the bombast of a bowel so welcome?
Who would have thought its haste through rushy glens,
its shotcrete slide of amplitude, its rocket plasma
and surge into the cool pool that is always protected by men
from the garnishees and gnashes of the mind,

who would have dreamt such quick-caught docking parts
to hold a matter so misshapen and yet so brave, so grave?
How its unsealed odor did break and sweat, relieving, unhousing
so much ill. It did not need the professional, nor the confessional.
Like gentle elves among the silver trodden leaves it was at home.

Leaf Falling

Full gold as the boundary's stand of birch,
russet as the oak will soon become,
leathered in swamp maple red,
do I fall, now, into my long prepared
ridiculously promising yellows, crisp skins, and crimson flaunts,
into pods and husks and locust pennies on the stone.

I have been green long enough,
rehearsing a production for numbers of the invisible pen,
required to rejoice as flowers fluttered on my fringe,
worked inexorably into seed thank God;
I leave and let the common green dream of rain,
cough up donations for the needs of autumnal shade.

Who is there to tell me why the birch
has let my gold come loose into a merely passing wind?
Who approves my pirouettes of style
dancing in homage to this frilly air?
Too shortly I'll be claimed with all the multitudes,
captured by stiff sward, spring pulse inert, too insect-busy to know flight.

I don't look down to destiny, I fly sideways, up
and away from home, I fly with multitudes flying,
astride the undying appetite of this tender breeze,
its teeth recovering from death-squad work;
now it rides itself to beauty and the law. Later, compulsively,
it will gnash again above the mulching fragments of our Selves.

continued

And we'll be done. But place no markers here.
Whatever we dared to offer will feed the next;
if poison, to be modified by rain,
if nourishment, to be expanded into plenitude and range.
Remembered, we merely translate into myth.
Forgotten, we change or live uproariously on.

House Of Phoebe

In the House of Phoebe

there is Sun Rising,
lifting from a crib
where myrtle protects

memory in fragile soil,
rising to the path
its chariot will follow,

rising to the clock by a stairs,
rising to the Room of Parents
where cattails and dogwhistle

double a night-song,
rising even to the attic,
to locks on trunks

and the murmur of birds
who nest summerwards,
chimneyswift, aerial, at home

even in strange places;
the Sun Rising Descends,
past locks and Parents and clock

to a room where music
slides off the mutes
of the written page,

becomes heard,
even downward the Sun Descends
to the Feast not yet,

not yet even planned for.

        *   *   *

And if, in the House of Phoebe

there is a Sun Rising,
and a Sun Setting,
and a Journey daily

from the basement
where all things
find their source,

there is also a Moon
whose vagaries are consequent
with apples and decline,

whose light
is adequate
in November's hush,

and there are Stars
rimming the china
of the flat universe,

there are stars yoked
in the folded curtains
of distress; there are all

such Furnishings of Heaven,
and there are as well,
the Common Things,

earth things, known
sometimes by visions.
In the House of Phoebe

will be all this forever.

Oh Breakfast!

Why so hard at the end?
Hard enough to get born

    though the freshened snake does not remember
    the skin that lies behind it in the grass.

And it's not as if there wasn't struggle,
loss and despair among our days of peace,

    and no, it's not as though we ask reward
    for making peace among the ruins,

of finding love in spite of loss. No, we accept:
death must win; but why with so much pain?

*   *   *

Why can't all of which we are composed
just shrink? Dim? Just suddenly be gone?

    Why must every organ, having played
    so beautifully in near silence for so long,

suddenly slam down the keys and howl,
bashing each other till the sounds

break through the sills and films
of flesh and drags these quarrels down to —

breakfast? Oh Breakfast! The lovely time when day
begins and no phone makes us sigh.

* * *

There is a spread of warmth, spring rain
of peaceful concentration,

      opening flowers and changing beacons
      in words we read, refuse to read, digest.

Oh breakfast! Unsullied by the day ahead,
and cleansed of yesterday.

      Now, in our achieved great age
      we're robbed of even breakfast.

Nurses and equipment jolt.
Needles are replaced.

* * *

The dead have been carried out.
We wait our turn. But then,

      would we really rather have been a snake?
      If chaos has enriched our lives,

and so much at stake, why not have equal pay
for equal life —

                — as now we stand and slowly break.

Copies of *Winter Ferry* can be ordered at:

- eelliott246@gmail.com
- The Bookstore: 413-637-3390
- Artisan Bindery: 207-734-6852
- Amazon.com

For more information and audio clips, visit our website at:

www.eelliottpoetry.com

ELIZABETH ELLIOTT

Winter Ferry is Elliott's fifth book of poetry. From 1976 to 1981 she taught the craft of poetry in the Gallatin Division of NYU, devising a system of fourteen ideograms as a means of comparing rhythms in English poetry, Chaucer through Ashbery.

With composer Seth Cooper, Elliott co-founded, and for a decade directed, an inter-disciplinary performing arts organization, Spectra. Some of Spectra's venues were Hudson, New York, Merkin Hall in New York City, and the Asia Society. In 1987 Spectra produced Elliott's ¡Cordoba!, a recreation of the world's first high civilization in which Jews, Moslems and Christians lived and worked as equals.

Elliott's first marriage was to Alexander Aldrich with whom she had four children. She is presently married to composer Clinton Elliott; they live in Maine, the Florida Keys and Tyringham, Massachusetts.

The cover is a detail of *The Way Home* by the American painter Evelina Kats, 1936-1999. There is a link to her work on *www.eelliottpoetry.com*

ACKNOWLEDGEMENTS

WB Yeats writes of the conflict between life and the work. I am grateful to the following people who stayed out of the way of the work but made its reality possible: Mary Zander who published *Burn All Night;* Kat Moran who has created this physical volume; Greg Steele who was the technical expert for the audio compact disc; Faith Englund and Diane Zeigler who created the website, Bill Dimbat, John Berthet and Jill Disser. Thank you all.

Then there are those who understand the conflict between life and work and insist on both, especially my husband, Clint.

Unsolicited letters from early readers of **Winter Ferry:**

I read it all in one sitting, handing it off to Polly saying, "Read this one!" I don't think I've ever read poetry with such eagerness to know "what next?"
    – **Susan Rodgers,** sculptor

To find a poet who has not abandoned the romance of language, who doesn't spend her time making sure she is severe is a great blessing for an old Victorian communist like me. And *Winter Ferry* itself is an important poem.
    – **Val Coleman,**
        writer and civil rights worker

The poetry always grabs me by the throat!
    – **Richard Lipez,**
        foreign affairs journalist and, as Richard Stevenson,
        author of gay mystery books

The only poem that in its overthrow of the paradigm, threw me over as well, was "In Praise," but I take that as an indication of my limitations. An Elizabethan (no pun intended) would find it joyful, as it clearly is.
    – **Alice Wohl,**
        independent scholar and translator of *Bellori's Lives*

The poems are strong. During the reading I felt pulled mentally and emotionally to extreme and different places. Recovery time would have been in order.
    – **Monica Zanen,** painter

Praise for **Crack in the Frame:**

Whether talking about love, sex, growing old, family, nature or obliquely about current politics, Elizabeth Elliott's elevated, almost archaic language, her elegiac tone and her piercing, relentless eye bring into stark relief the angst and quandaries of the post-modern age. She is always in control of cadence and syntax. Her love of sound as well as sense sings through the urgency of these poems.
    – **David Budbill,** poet